What Kind (

CW01500983

A musical

by

Roy Smiles

Featuring the songs of Anthony Newley & Leslie Bricusse

What Kind Of Fool?

Cast

A play for a cast of six:

ANTHONY NEWLEY
THE DEVIL

All other characters played by the same actors:

GRACIE NEWLEY
GEORGE PICAUD
PETER USTINOV
AN ARMY OFFICER
A SERGEANT MAJOR
LESLIE BRICUSSE
JOAN COLLINS
NORMAN WISDOM
REX HARRISON
MILTON BERLE
AN AMERICAN AGENT
A CHARLIE CHAPLIN.

Staging

A stage in the shape and style of a circus ring.

Dedicated to

Newberg & Brickman.

Songs

Act One

'The Joker' (Newley/Bricusse)
'Pop Goes The Weasel' (Trad./Newley)
'Feeling Good' (Newley/Bricusse)
'Strawberry Fair' (Trad./Newley)
'Gonna Build A Mountain' (Newley/Bricusse)
'Look At That Face' Bricusse)
'On A Wonderful Day Like Today' (Newley/Bricusse)
'Beautiful Things' (Bricusse)
'Life Is A Woman' (Bricusse)
'Who Can I Turn Too?' (Newley/Bricusse)

Act Two

'Once In A Lifetime' (Newley/Bricusse)
'Pure Imagination' (Newley/Bricusse)
'The Good Old Bad Old Days' (Newley/Bricusse)
'The Good Things In Life' (Newley/Bricusse)
'I'll Begin Again' (Bricusse)
'The Joker - Reprise' (Newley/Bricusse)
'What Kind Of Fool Am I?' (Newley/Bricusse)

Act One

The lights rise on:

A sawdust strewn stage: in the style of a circus ring.

The overall tone of the set should be half vaudeville/half avant-garde.

A spotlight focuses on: ANTHONY NEWLEY.

He is dressed (without the white-face) as 'Littlechap', his character from 'Stop The World (I Want To Get Off)'. He sings: 'The Joker' to the audience:

The Joker

NEWLEY.   There's always a Joker in the pack
There's always a cardboard clown
The poor painted fool falls on his back
And everyone laughs when he's down.

There's always a funny man in the game
But he's only funny by mistake
But everyone laughs at him, just the same
They don't see his painted heart break.

They don't care as long as there is a jester, just a fool
As foolish as he can be
There's always a Joker, that's a rule
But fate deals the hand and I see
The Joker is me.

There's always a funny man in the game
But he's only funny by mistake
But everyone laughs at him, just the same
They don't see his painted heart break.

They don't care as long as there is a jester, just a fool
As foolish as he can be
There's always a Joker, that's a rule
But fate deals the hand and I see
The Joker is me
The Joker is me
The Joker is me.

The song finishes. Lights rise on the circus ring stage.

The DEVIL enters. He wears a red suit & is wildly raffish.

DEVIL.	Evening.
NEWLEY.	You're late.
DEVIL.	I am?
NEWLEY.	Lateness equals rudeness. That's what my old Grandmother used to say. Mind you, she was a drooling simpleton.
DEVIL.	I do apologise, I was busy forking Mormons.
NEWLEY.	For marrying more than one wife?
DEVIL.	No, just for being Mormons, shall we begin?
NEWLEY.	*(Mock surprise)* We haven't begun?
DEVIL.	I would have noticed. Why not begin at the beginning?
NEWLEY.	That's such a dull theatrical convention.
DEVIL.	Where would you start, at the end?
NEWLEY.	Couldn't we begin in the middle?
DEVIL.	It'll confuse the public.
NEWLEY.	*(Laughs)* My musicals always confused the public.
DEVIL.	But I hate flashbacks.
NEWLEY.	Why so?
DEVIL.	All that mist, it's very off-putting.
NEWLEY.	Very well, if you insist. *(Calls off)* Unleash the common horde.

The other CAST members enter as East End characters from the 1930's.

DEVIL.	*(Aside)* Who are all these terrible people?
NEWLEY.	The working classes.
DEVIL.	I was wondering about the smell.
NEWLEY.	That's the East End for you: all arm-pit. I was born in Hackney.
DEVIL.	Hackney?

NEWLEY.	You couldn't move for the clogs and consumption.
DEVIL.	Sounds scenic.
NEWLEY.	But though we were poor - we were miserable.
DEVIL.	But of course.
NEWLEY.	Saturday night's highlight was the mass grope around the back of the Hackney Empire.
DEVIL.	*(Keen)* Groping? There was groping?
NEWLEY.	*(Calls off)* Could you fetch some bromide for Satan? *(Beat)* Where was I?
DEVIL.	Grovelling in your own filth midst the urban proletariat?
NEWLEY.	That was it, the 1930's. Of course, in those days, the East End had a language of its own.
DEVIL.	Etruscan?
NEWLEY.	Harder to translate: cockney rhyming slang. There was Butcher's Hook: crook. Apples and Pears: stairs. Boxer's Mitt: git.
DEVIL.	You seem to be speaking in tongues.
NEWLEY.	Someone has too. You wouldn't believe the words they made up. Take a weasel -
DEVIL.	Isn't that a glorified ferret?
NEWLEY.	Not in the least, not in the East End. Oh no -

NEWLEY starts to sing 'Pop Goes The Weasel.' The CAST sing with him:

Pop Goes The Weasel

NEWLEY
& CAST.

Half a pound of tuppenny rice
Half a pound of treacle
That's the way the money goes
Pop goes the weasel.

NEWLEY & CAST.	Every night, when I go out The weasel's on the table Take a stick and knock it off Pop goes the weasel. Up and down the city road In and out of the eagle That's the way the money goes Pop goes the weasel. Half a pound of tuppenny rice Half a pound of treacle Mix it up and make it nice Pop goes the weasel.
NEWLEY.	*(Speaks)* You know, pop goes the weasel For years, I've wondered What that meant And nobody seemed to know So, I looked it up And the official explanation Goes something like this: Pop goes the weasel refers to The habit of London hatters long ago Popping or pawning their weasels Or accessories on Saturday night To buy liquor, isn't that interesting?
DEVIL.	Not really.
NEWLEY & CAST.	*(Sings)* Up and down the city road In and out of the eagle That's the way the money goes Pop goes the weasel.
NEWLEY.	*(Speaks)* But you know I've got a theory of my own About pop goes the weasel It's much simpler:

NEWLEY
& CAST.   *(Sings)* Why did the weasel go pop, go pop
                 Pop, pop goes the weasel
                 Why did the weasel go pop
                 'Cause they upped the price
                 Of tuppeny rice to four pence.

                 How did the pop get into the weasel
                 Weasel, pop goes the weasel
                 How did the pop get in there
                 Well, the weasel caught his
                 Beakle in the treacle.

                 Now, if you've got a weasel
                 And you don't want him to pop
                 The next time you go shopping
                 Don't you take him in the shop
                 Two, three, four.
                 Half a pound of tuppenny rice
                 Half a pound of treacle
                 Now that is the way
                 That the money goes
                 Pop goes the weasel.

                 Every night, when I go out
                 The weasel's sitting on the table
                 Now I take a stick
                 And I knock it off
                 Pop goes the weasel.

                 Up and down the city road
                 In and out of the eagle
                 That's the way the money goes
                 Pop goes the weasel.
                 Together now:
                 Half a pound of tuppenny rice
                 Half a pound of treacle
                 Now, I mix it up
                 And I make it nice
                 Pop, pop, pop goes the weasel
                 Pop, pop, pop goes the weasel
                 Poppity, poppity, pop
                 Goes the weasel now.

The song ends, the CAST exit.

DEVIL.	So how was the Depression?
NEWLEY.	*(Sour)* Depressing, I can't think why.
DEVIL.	And your family, cockneys all I presume?
NEWLEY.	*(Nods)* My mother was Jewish, my father wasn't.
DEVIL.	You're only half Jewish?
NEWLEY.	Yes, but in my defence, it's the top half.
DEVIL.	What was the bottom half?
NEWLEY.	Pure Philistine.
DEVIL.	That would explain a lot.
NEWLEY.	You're telling me. My Dad slung his hook.
DEVIL.	He had a hook, was he a pirate?
NEWLEY.	No, just twice as shifty; he left home, giggling. I was brought up by my Mum. All on her own save for my Gran and a hundred and forty-seven aunties. Crowded? There wasn't room enough to swing a budgie. To cheer things up the powers that be decided to have a war.
DEVIL.	Any particular one?
NEWLEY.	World War Two; they later turned it into a film with John Mills: all kit-bags, concentration camps and cocoa.
DEVIL.	It rings a distant bell.
NEWLEY.	I was packed off to the countryside.
DEVIL.	How invigorating.
NEWLEY.	Where I was sadistically beaten by village idiots of all shapes and sizes.
DEVIL.	It's the country code.
NEWLEY.	I returned to London when the bombs stopped falling.
DEVIL.	At least you thought they had.

NEWLEY.   Yes, the V1's and V2's were still to come. Nice Mr. Hitler's last nasty surprise.

DEVIL.   I have Israelis stoning him with bagels as we speak.

NEWLEY.   Make sure they're rock hard.

Enter GRACIE NEWLEY, Newley's mother, dressed in World War Two clothes.

DEVIL.   Who's the old crone?

GRACIE.   *(To Devil)* Who you calling an old crone?

DEVIL.   Who's the young crone?

GRACIE.   That's better.

NEWLEY.   It's my Mum, Gracie. *(Child's tone)* Hello Mum.

GRACIE.   Where you been?

NEWLEY.   I was evacuated, Mum, remember? You put me on a train.

GRACIE.   What else could I do?

NEWLEY.   Not a lot with the Luftwaffe coming in droves.

GRACIE.   The Germans had to bomb us?

NEWLEY.   They bombed the whole of the East End, Mum.

GRACIE.   Right, because it's Jewish.

NEWLEY.   No, Mum, 'cause of the docks.

GRACIE.   Keep telling yourself that, boy.

NEWLEY.   It's not personal, Mum, its war.

GRACIE.   Trust me, boy, it's always personal.

NEWLEY.   What, you think they're only bombing Jewish houses?

GRACIE.   If they could, they would.

NEWLEY.   Where you going?

GRACIE.   To queue.

NEWLEY.   For what?

GRACIE.   Spam.

NEWLEY.   *(Laughs)* Spam, hasn't that got pork in it?

GRACIE.   If it means eating we're suddenly Protestant.

GRACIE exits.

DEVIL.   Rationing: it never caught on.

NEWLEY.   I wonder why? Back to the Doodlebugs.

DEVIL.   Such a charming name for weapons of such destruction.

NEWLEY.   When they started falling I was sent to Morecambe in Lancashire: city of banjos, kiss-me-quick hats and donkey poo.

DEVIL.   And mass fondling under the pier.

NEWLEY.   Only on Bank Holidays. *(Calls off)* Double that dose of bromide. *(Beat)* I ended up staying with a bloke called George Pescud: a lovely old cove, who'd been a music hall entertainer; I found the stories he told about show-business absolutely fascinating.

Enter GEORGE PESCUD, a vaudeville entertainer.

NEWLEY.   Hello George.

GEORGE.   Hey-up, lad.

NEWLEY.   How's death?

GEORGE.   A bit like the Glasgow Empire on a Friday night.

NEWLEY.   Survived that one myself.

GEORGE.   If you can survive the Glasgow Empire you can survive anything, lad.

NEWLEY.   It never scared me; it was just Hackney with haggis.

GEORGE.   *(Laughs)* That's it, son, Hackney with haggis.

NEWLEY.   George here filled me with showbiz dreams.

GEORGE.   You did me proud, old son.

NEWLEY.   And also gave me a lifetime's supply of really bad jokes.

GEORGE.   I say, I say, I say.

NEWLEY.   What do you say?

GEORGE.   Why do cream crackers hate jazz?

NEWLEY.   I don't know why do cream crackers hate jazz?

GEORGE.   Because they're square.

NEWLEY.   I say, I say, I say.

GEORGE,   What do you say?

NEWLEY.   What do you call a man with jelly in one ear and custard in the other?

GEORGE.   I don't know, what do you call a man with jelly in one ear and custard in the other?

NEWLEY.   A trifle deaf.

GEORGE exits. The DEVIL gives NEWLEY an arch look.

NEWLEY.   Well I didn't say he was bright.

DEVIL.   I'd take him myself but with those jokes I'd make a hell of my own.

NEWLEY.   He filled my head with stories of the great times I'd have in showbiz and all the girls I'd meet. There'd be money and girls and fame and glory and more girls. Did I mention the girls?

DEVIL.   You mentioned the girls. Who needs the bromide, me or you?

NEWLEY.   I came back to the East End when the war was over.

DEVIL.   Or what was left of it.

NEWLEY.   (Noel Coward voice) Ah, but the rubble looked so beautiful in the moonlight.

DEVIL.   It improved the neighbourhood.

NEWLEY.   I couldn't believe the shooting had stopped. It was going to be a brave new world.

DEVIL.   And no more war.

NEWLEY.   So they believed.

DEVIL.   What fools mankind were to dream that?

NEWLEY.   Ah, but it was a fine dream.

The CAST enter in V.E Night clothing and sing: 'Feeling Good.' The DEVIL and NEWLEY watch.

Feeling Good

CAST.   Birds flying high you know how I feel
             Sun in the sky you know how I feel
             Reeds drifting on by you know how I feel
             It's a new dawn, it's a new day
             It's a new life for me
             And I'm feeling good.

             Fish in the sea you know how I feel
             River running free you know how I feel
             Blossom in the tree you know how I feel
             It's a new dawn, it's a new day
             It's a new life for me
             And I'm feeling good.

             Dragonfly out in the sun you know what I mean
             Butterflies all having fun you know what I mean
             Sleep in peace when the day is done, that's what I mean
             And this old world is a new world, and a bold world
             For me, for me.

             Stars when you shine you know how I feel
             Scent of the pine you know how I feel
             Yeah freedom is mine and I know how I feel
             It's a new dawn, it's a new day
             It's a new life, it's a new dawn
             It's a new day, it's a new life
             For me and I'm feeling good.

The song ends. The CAST exit.

DEVIL.   Thus you were back in the East End.

NEWLEY.   Broke as per but I knew, even then, I had to get out and get out fast.

13

DEVIL.	Through a life of crime?
NEWLEY.	Too cowardly.
DEVIL.	A career in football?
NEWLEY.	Two left feet.
DEVIL.	Then how?
NEWLEY.	On that I hadn't got a Danny La Rue.
DEVIL.	You left school early.
NEWLEY.	Yes.
DEVIL.	Were you academically remedial?
NEWLEY.	I never took to school. I never saw the point. I left at fourteen and was marking time working as a tea-boy to help my mother out. She was taking in washing. The place stank of it, you couldn't move for laundry.
DEVIL.	Aren't you overdoing this poverty shtick, old boy?
NEWLEY.	If you think I'm over egging it ask her.

GRACIE, his mother, enters wearily with a basket of washing.

GRACIE.	Hello? I spent more time between sheets than Warren bloody Beatty.

She exits.

NEWLEY.	We were saved by an ad for child actors at the Italia Conti stage school.
DEVIL.	Fancy.
NEWLEY.	I went along and they offered me a place. But it was twenty guineas a term. I said: 'we haven't got twenty bleedin' shillings.' But they liked me so much they said I could be a tea-boy there while I studied.
DEVIL.	Back to making tea?

NEWLEY.   Always: tasted like gorilla pee my cuppa but no-one seemed to mind. I was on my way. I did a Saturday morning children series called *Dusty Bates*. Then I was discovered by Peter Ustinov.

DEVIL.   Him that fiddled as Nero, in *Quo Vadis*?

NEWLEY.   While Rome burned.

Enter PETER USTINOV, dressed as the Emperor Nero.

NEWLEY.   Speaking of fiddling: Mr. Ustinov.

USTINOV.   Hello small boy.

NEWLEY.   Who you calling small?

USTINOV.   Do you think you could play an adult?

NEWLEY.   I haven't yet but I'll give anything a go once.

USTINOV.   Would you like to be in my film *Visa Versa*?

NEWLEY.   I'd like to be in anything.

USTINOV.   It's about a father and son who exchange identities.

NEWLEY.   Sounds painful but if gets my mother out of washing sheets I'm your boy.

USTINOV.   Feel free not to wash sheets during filming.

NEWLEY.   Aren't you of Russian, German and Ethiopian descent?

USTINOV.   Via Swiss Cottage but only on my father's side; my mother was of Russian and Italian ancestry. She believed in revolution but only if the restaurants improved. One of her ancestors was chef to Tsar Paul.

NEWLEY.   That's nice.

USTINOV.   It didn't stop her burning soup. You had to bring two things to my mother's dinner parties: a good wine and a stomach-pump.

NEWLEY.   We couldn't see the soup in our house for the blinding whiteness of the washing.

USTINOV.   *(Sighs)* Self-pity isn't just for Christmas - it's for life.

NEWLEY.   In our neighbourhood they cancelled Christmas: just after Santa got stabbed by urchins.

USTINOV.   *(Winces)* It's always fascinating meeting the lower orders.

USTINOV exits.

NEWLEY.   *Visa Versa* was a hit and the director David Lean saw it.

DEVIL.   Him that directed *Lawrence Of Arabia*?

NEWLEY.   That's the boy. Before he spent quality time with camels he filmed Dickens stories, a nice working class boy himself.

DEVIL.   Lean?

NEWLEY.   Dickens.

DEVIL.   You're obsessed with class.

NEWLEY.   I'm English, who isn't?

DEVIL.   Well, I've never bothered.

NEWLEY.   Satan is English?

DEVIL.   Only according to the Irish.

NEWLEY.   Anyway, I got the part of a lifetime: playing the Artful Dodger in *Oliver Twist*.

DEVIL.   A professional cockney from the start?

NEWLEY.   More an enthusiastic amateur; Alec Guinness played Fagin. I was learning at the feet of giants.

DEVIL.   A child actor, it explains much.

NEWLEY.   There's a problem?

DEVIL.   They never grow up, you know.

NEWLEY.   I'd disagree but when you're right, you're right. The film was a huge hit all around the world. Save for America where they said Guinness's Fagin was anti-Semitic.

DEVIL.   No shit Shylock.

GRACIE enters.

GRACIE.   With your success I gave up the washing.

NEWLEY.   You never had to work again.

GRACIE.   Who knew you mucking about in front of a camera would change our lives?

NEWLEY.   'Mucking about'? It's called acting, Mum.

GRACIE.   You weren't acting as Dodger. You were him.

NEWLEY.   True.

GRACIE.   Shame about that Nancy: shouldn't happen to a dog.

GRACIE exits.

NEWLEY.   Due to my role as Dodger the Rank Organisation put me under a seven year film contract. Alas, most of the films were rank.

DEVIL.   Why the contempt?

NEWLEY.   I always played the same part: the cheery cockney squaddie in stiff upper lipped war films. With dialogue like: 'cup of Bovril, Captain?'

A British ARMY CAPTAIN enters. Very stiff upper lipped.

CAPTAIN.   Don't mind if I do. Chalky White isn't it?

NEWLEY.   That's right, sir. *(Salutes)* Working Class Stereotype No. 314.

CAPTAIN.   What'll you do when this war is over, Chalky?

NEWLEY.   Go back to the East End with my Bovril, sir.

CAPTAIN.   Capital.

NEWLEY.   Marry my childhood sweetheart, open that whelk shop I always wanted to open.

CAPTAIN. Good show.

NEWLEY. Sow pearls on my jacket, stab policemen, have children with built in lice, that sort of thing, sir.

CAPTAIN. Damn good show.

NEWLEY. Shall I touch my forelock now or later, sir?

CAPTAIN. As soon as you've been shot will be fine. *(Beat)* Quiet isn't it?

NEWLEY. Too quiet, sir.

CAPTAIN. Wonder what Jerry is up too?

NEWLEY. Probably conceiving fiendish ways to kill minor cockney characters in World War Two war films, sir, after all, the working classes are expendable.

CAPTAIN. I just want you to know Chalky, and I am being patronising here let me make that patently clear, if you don't make it home you're the salt of the earth.

NEWLEY. Thank you, Captain.

CAPTAIN. And though, as soon as this war is over, I plan never to speak to anyone working class again, if I'm ever passing that whelk shop of yours in my Bentley -

NEWLEY. You'll pop in, sir?

CAPTAIN. No but, my God, I'll wave.

NEWLEY. God bless you Captain, cup of Bovril, Captain?

CAPTAIN. Thought you'd never ask, Chalky.

The ARMY CAPTAIN salutes and exits.

DEVIL. I see your point.

NEWLEY. Rank sacked me when they found me under a piano at a Rank cocktail party with Diana Dors.

DEVIL. What were you doing under a piano with Diana Dors?

NEWLEY.   I was helping her remove a peanut that had fallen down her cleavage.

DEVIL.   Naked?

NEWLEY.   Naturally, well, Diana Dors, wouldn't you?

His mother GRACIE enters:

GRACIE.   You were a dirty little toe-rag. What were you?

NEWLEY.   A dirty little toe-rag, Mum.

GRACIE.   And you never changed.

NEWLEY.   Not now Mum, I'm attempting to look heroic.

GRACIE.   In those trousers?

NEWLEY.   *(To audience)* My mother, folks: living proof you can choose your friends but your family will always embarrass you.

GRACIE.   Are you going to mention prison?

NEWLEY.   I was getting to it.

His mother GRACIE exits.

NEWLEY.   *(Stares after her)* I should have been adopted.

DEVIL.   Prison?

NEWLEY.   Brixton Nick, always a joy.

DEVIL.   You went to prison for having sex under a piano?

NEWLEY.   I got done for driving without my licence.

DEVIL.   You desperate character you.

NEWLEY.   The judge decided to make an example of me. Oddly enough I met a better class of person in prison than I ever did in Hackney. I got really good at pottery. I was building an escape ladder out of clay when my sentence was up. I was released a sadder, wiser and thinner person.

DEVIL.   Still, at least you survived.

NEWLEY.	I can't believe I did because I went to pieces in the army. My acting career was just taking off when I got called up for National Service.
DEVIL.	National Service: teaching juvenile delinquents to be better men by going abroad and shooting strangers.
NEWLEY.	They should bring it back, he lied.

A SERGEANT-MAJOR enters and yells:

SERGEANT-MAJOR.	You're a horrible little man, Newley, what are you?
NEWLEY.	It's a long shot, sergeant, but I'm a horrible little man?
SERGEANT-MAJOR.	We could be at war with Russia any day and you're late on parade.
NEWLEY.	If the Russians want the East End they can have it. Mind you, they'll have a fight on their hands. You can get mugged in a tank.
SERGEANT-MAJOR.	Call yourself a soldier?
NEWLEY.	I call myself a sissy but you can call me what you like, you're bigger than me.
SERGEANT-MAJOR.	And where's your bleeding rifle?
NEWLEY.	I swapped it for some curtains.
SERGEANT-MAJOR.	You're not fit for the British Army.
NEWLEY.	I've been telling you that for weeks.
SERGEANT-MAJOR.	Right, dishonourable discharge.
NEWLEY.	Isn't that a form of self-abuse?

The SERGEANT-MAJOR exits.

NEWLEY.   I had a complete and utter breakdown. I realised I could no more be a soldier than fly to the moon. Ironic then I got my adult break in the film *Idol On Parade*, playing a National Serviceman. I played a pop singer of the Elvis variety who's called up into the army.

DEVIL.   Elvis, you?

NEWLEY.   The cut-price Woolworths variety; they thought we should have some songs. I sang them and when the movie came up I found myself a bona fida pop star with screaming fans to match. I became a singer by mistake.

DEVIL.   'Life's what happens to you in between making plans.' That's what John Lennon said.

NEWLEY.   Just before they shot him, but I was on my way. I was a teenyboppers delight on a Saturday night and every night of the year.

THE CAST make teenybopper girls piercing screams.

NEWLEY.   *(To audience)* Goes straight through you, doesn't it?

NEWLEY sings: 'Strawberry Fair.' The CAST enter and join:

Strawberry Fair

NEWLEY.   Strawberries, ripe strawberries
As I was going to Strawberry Fair
Singing, singing, butter-cups and daisies
I met a maiden selling her wares
Fol-de-dee!

Her eyes were blue and she was fair
And she rode on a donkey to Strawberry Fair
Ri-fol, ri-fol, tol-de-riddle-li-do
Ri-fol, ri-fol, tol-de-riddle-dee.

Would you like to pick from my basket, she said,
Singing, singing, Butter-cups and Daisies
My cherries ripe, or my roses red
Fol-de-dee!

You can take a handful, I don't care
As I go on to Strawberry Fair.
Ri-fol, ri-fol, tol-de-riddle-li-do
Ri-fol, ri-fol, tol-de-riddle-dee.

NEWLEY.   *(Cont)* So I said to this bird:
               Your cherries soon will go mouldy and bad
               Singing, singing buttercups and wotsits
               Your roses wither and look all sad
               Fol-de-dee!

               Now it's not to buy such perishing ware
               That I am slogging it to Strawberry Fair
               Oh, ri-fol, ri-fol, come and get an earful
               Ri-fol, ri-fol, tol-de-riddle-dee.

               I told her straight:
               I want a girl with a generous heart
               Singing, singing, butter-cups and oojahs
               Without a tongue that is wicked or smart
               Fol-de-dee!

               And an honest mind, but these are rare
               I doubt if I'll find them at this crummy old fair
               Ri-fol, ri-fol, tol-de-riddle-li-do
               Ri-fol, well, you know the rest, don't you?

               So I put it to her straight:
               Now in return for these virtues, I swear
               Knees up, knees up, come and have a knees up
               I'll give you a ring for your finger my dear
               Fol-de-dee!

               So make me your partner and give me a share
               In church today at Strawberry Fair
               Now, ri-fol, ri-fol, tol-de-riddle-li-do
               Ri-fol, ri-fol -
               Strawberries, shan't be round tomorrow
               The donkey's pinched all the strawberries
               Hee-hee-hee-hee.

The song ends, the CAST exit.

DEVIL.   Was that one hundred percent, authentic, pseudo-cockney gibberish?

NEWLEY.   You noticed.

LESLIE BRICUSSE enters, a young songwriter.

BRICUSSE.   Are you going to mention me at all?

NEWLEY. Brickman.

BRICUSSE. Newberg.

DEVIL. Who's this?

NEWLEY. My writing partner: Leslie Bricusse, the lad himself.

BRICUSSE. A legend in my own bathroom.

NEWLEY. When I first met you, you were a 25 year old wunderkind.

BRICUSSE. We were joined at the hip straight away.

NEWLEY. You called me Newberg.

BRICUSSE. You called me Brickman.

NEWLEY. We were supposed to write a fifteen minute show.

BRICUSSE. For you to do on tour.

NEWLEY. In between my hits.

BRICUSSE. You were getting bored singing them.

NEWLEY. And all the screaming; I felt a fake.

BRICUSSE. It turned into a full show.

NEWLEY. We did it in Manchester.

BRICUSSE. *Stop The World - I Want To Get Off.*

NEWLEY. *(To the Devil)* Picture it if you will. A circus arena -

DEVIL. *(Sour)* I think I can manage that.

NEWLEY. I played an everyman, asking questions about life, and love.

BRICUSSE. 'Littlechap.'

NEWLEY. That was me.

BRICUSSE. And his journey to find himself.

NEWLEY. A journey I never completed.

BRICUSSE.   Not in real life.

NEWLEY.   The show was arty.

BRICUSSE.   It was strange.

NEWLEY.   The critics didn't know whether to love it loathe it.

BRICUSSE.   *(Laughs)* But they finally snapped into action and decided to loathe it.

NEWLEY.   But the public still came in droves.

BRICUSSE.   It was a hit.

NEWLEY.   A sensation.

BRICUSSE.   We reached the West End.

NEWLEY.   And it ran for years.

BRICUSSE.   There were turning the crowds away.

NEWLEY.   You found more fame.

BRICUSSE.   And women.

NEWLEY.   They came in droves too.

BRICUSSE.   A triumph for Newley & Bricusse.

NEWLEY.   Brickman & Newberg.

BRICUSSE.   Song-smith's extraordinaire.

NEWLEY.   We'd reached the mountain top.

BRICUSSE.   And seen the Promised Land.

NEWLEY sings 'Gonna Build Me A Mountain.'

Gonna Build Me A Mountain

NEWLEY.   I'm gonna build a mountain from a little hill
I'm gonna build a mountain, least I hope I will
I'm gonna build a mountain, I'm gonna build it high
I don't know how I'm gonna do it, only know I'm gonna try.

NEWLEY.   *(Cont)* I'm gonna build a daydream, from a little hope
I'm gonna push the daydream, up that mountain slope
I'm gonna build a daydream, I'm gonna see it through.

Gonna build a mountain and a daydream
Gonna make them both come true.
I'm gonna build a heaven, and I will someday
And the Lord Sends Gabriel to take me away
Woah I wanna fine young son to take my place
I'll leave my son in my heaven on earth with the good Lord's grace.

I'm gonna build a mountain from a little hill
I'm gonna build a mountain, least I hope I will
I'm gonna build a mountain, I'm gonna build it high
I don't know how I'm gonna do it, only know I'm gonna try.
I'm gonna build a daydream, from a little hope
I'm gonna push the daydream, up that mountain slope
I'm gonna build a daydream, I'm gonna see it through
Gonna build a mountain and a daydream
Gonna make them both come true.

I'm gonna build a heaven, and I will someday
And the Lord Sends Gabriel to take me away
Woah I wanna fine young son to take my place
I'll leave my son in my heaven on earth with the good Lord's grace.

The song finishes. BRICUSSE salutes him and exits.

DEVIL.   You make conquering the West End sound like Everest.

NEWLEY.   Trust me: conquering the West End is harder.

DEVIL.   Where's your ice-pick?

NEWLEY.   My Mum's just knitting me one.

Enter JOAN COLLINS, Newley's second wife.

JOAN.   Newley.

NEWLEY.   Joanie.

JOAN.   I think it's time I got a mention don't you?

NEWLEY.   I didn't mention the first wife.

JOAN.   Yes, shame on you.

NEWLEY.   I didn't behave very well.

JOAN.   You were a rotter.

NEWLEY.   But I knew it.

JOAN.   Then came me.

NEWLEY.   You were the international film star: Miss Joan Collins.

JOAN.   Fed up of Hollywood.

NEWLEY.   They didn't know what to do with you.

JOAN.   I came to see the show.

NEWLEY.   You'd got tired of Warren Beatty.

JOAN.   He'd tire anyone out. We'd been engaged.

DEVIL.   Didn't you used to have sex with him six times a day?

JOAN.   *(Laughs)* He did, I just lay there, darling.

NEWLEY.   You thought I was a big head.

JOAN.   You kept me waiting twenty minutes.

NEWLEY.   I told Joyce Blair I fancied you rotten.

JOAN.   Because you did.

NEWLEY.   You fancied me.

JOAN.   Rotten right back.

NEWLEY.   It was lust at first sight.

JOAN.   The love came after.

NEWLEY.   We blew hot and cold.

JOAN.   I started seeing Terence Stamp.

NEWLEY.   I was jealous.

JOAN.   You couldn't commit.

NEWLEY.   I told you I could never stay faithful.

JOAN.   The only promise you ever kept.

NEWLEY.   It was heaven.

JOAN.   And hell.

NEWLEY.   And all things in between.

JOAN.   Mr. Chalk and Mrs. Cheese.

NEWLEY.   But magical.

JOAN.   Always.

NEWLEY sings to JOAN: 'Look At That Face.'

Look At That Face

NEWLEY.   Look at that face
           Just look at it
           Look at that fabulous face of yours
           I knew first look I took at it
           This was the face that the world adores.

           Look at those eyes
           As wise and as deep as the sea
           Look at that nose
           It shows what a nose should be.
           As for your smile, it's lyrical
           Friendly and warm as a summer's day
           That face is just a miracle
           Where could I ever find words to say.

           The way that it makes me happy
           Whatever the time or place?
           I'll find in no book
           What I find when I look
           At that face.

JOAN joins.

NEWLEY
& JOAN. Look at that face
Just look at it
Look at that funny old face of yours
I knew first look I took at it
You've got a face like a kitchen door's.

Look at those eyes
As close as the closest of friends
Look at that nose
It starts where a good nose ends.

To say that there's no one like you
Would not even state the case
No wonder I shook
When I first took a look
At that face.

The song ends.

JOAN. When you sang you were perfection.

NEWLEY. It was when I wasn't singing I got into trouble.

JOAN. Don't I know it, darling?

JOAN exits.

DEVIL. How did a man like you get a woman like that?

NEWLEY. I laughed her into bed.

DEVIL. Was she still laughing in bed?

NEWLEY. Funny. *(Beat)* Sammy Davis Junior came to see the show. He wanted to record *What Kind Of Fool*. It sold a million copies. *Stop The World* got a transfer to Broadway, I was the toast of New York. Joan and I had the time of our lives. It was the swinging Sixties after all.

DEVIL. You know what they say: if you can remember the Sixties, you're a boring berk.

NEWLEY. Cynic; even the Bond producers came calling. They wanted a song for their film *Goldfinger*. John Barry did the music. I'd hoped they wanted me as Bond.

DEVIL.   *(Laughs)* A Jewish Bond? Oh, I don't think so.

NEWLEY.   Hey, we can shoot people. Look at the Israeli Army. They'll shoot anyone.

DEVIL.   So I've heard.

NEWLEY.   When *Stop The World* finished we started on another show, a burlesque on class.

DAVIL.   Your favourite subject.

NEWLEY.   The plot went as follows: Cocky -

DEVIL.   You?

NEWLEY.   You guessed - is a member of the lower class of society, who are governed by the elite. This upper class is represented by Sir, who has supreme power over Cocky, and those of his ilk. Cocky then comes across a character called 'the Negro', who convinces him to stand up to the upper class. After Cocky confronts Sir, they agree to share power, in order for the two classes to survive.

DEVIL.   Was it as pretentious as it sounds?

NEWLEY.   *(Laughs)* Pretentious? Moi? Au contraire. We called the show: *The Roar Of The Greasepaint, The Smell Of The Crowd.* Clever title what?

DEVIL.   Too clever by half.

NEWLEY.   They'll write that on my gravestone.

DEVIL.   Allow me.

NEWLEY.   I wasn't going to be in it, I was just going to direct. We got Norman Wisdom to play Cocky.

NORMAN WISDOM enters, trips over, shouts 'Mr. Grimsdale!' and sprawls to the floor.

NEWLEY.   But Norman overdid the pathos.

DEVIL.   Who knew?

WISDOM stands and exits, looking crest-fallen, with the maximum of pathos.

NEWLEY.   So I stepped into the role. We took it to America. Tony Bennett had already had a huge hit with *Who Can I Turn To*. So the audiences came to the show humming the tune. We sold out on tour and hit Broadway like a tornado.

The CAST enter and join NEWLEY as he sings:

On A Wonderful Day Like Today

NEWLEY
& CAST.   On a wonderful day like today,
I defy any cloud to appear in the sky,
Dare any raindrop to plop in my eye
On a wonderful day like today.

On a wonderful morning like this
When the sun is as big as a yellow balloon;
Even the sparrows are signing in tune
On a wonderful morning like this.

On a morning like this I could kiss everybody,
I'm so full of love and good will.
Let me say furthermore, I'd adore everybody
To come and dine, the pleasure's mine
And I will play the bill.

May I take this occasion to say
That the whole human race
Should go down on its knees
Show that we're grateful

For mornings like these
For the world's in a wonderful way
On a wonderful day like today.

On a wonderful day like today
When the sky is as grey as an elephants' nose,
Half of me's freezing - the other half's froze!

On a wonderful day like today - I'm only joking!
May I take this occasion to pray
For a little less cold and a little more heat.
Even the sparrows are stamping their feet;
If they spoke I know just what they'd say!
On a wonderful day like today.

The song ends. The CAST exit.

DEVIL.   So you were the toast of Broadway.

NEWLEY.   Married to one of the most beautiful women in the world, I had it all.

DEVIL.   Save children.

NEWLEY.   But Joan sorted that out, though I like to think I had a hand in it.

DEVIL.   More than a hand.

NEWLEY.   Sauce-box. Her name was Tara. I was the father of a baby girl.

JOAN enters carrying a baby.

JOAN.   I never thought you'd find the time.

NEWLEY.   To do what?

JOAN.   Get me pregnant.

NEWLEY.   I was never that busy.

JOAN.   You lived for the theatre.

NEWLEY.   It consumed me.

JOAN.   To the exclusion of everything else.

NEWLEY.   Sometimes, but not my children.

JOAN.   No. You can hold her, you know.

NEWLEY.   I'll break her.

JOAN.   She's not made of glass. *(Laughs)* Imagine, you a father.

NEWLEY.   Imagine.

JOAN.   She looked like you.

NEWLEY.   No, more like you. *(To baby)* Hello.

JOAN.   Sing to her.

NEWLEY.   She won't understand.

JOAN.   Trust me, she'll understand.

He holds the baby and stares into its face, they begins to sing softly: 'Beautiful Things'

Beautiful Things

NEWLEY.   The world is full of beautiful things
            Butterfly wings, fairy tale kings
            And each new day undoubtedly brings
            Still more beautiful things.

            The world abounds with many delights
            Magical sights, fanciful flights
            And those who dream on beautiful nights
            Dream of beautiful things.

            Beautiful days of for sunshine lazing
            Beautiful skies and shores
            Beautiful days when I can gaze
            In beautiful eyes - like yours.

            Our lives tick by like pendulum swings
            Poor little things, puppets on strings
            Life is full of beautiful things
            Beautiful people too
            Beautiful people like you.

            The world is full of beautiful things
            Butterfly wings, fairy tale kings
            And each new day undoubtedly brings
            Still more beautiful things.

            The world abounds with many delights
            Magical sights, fanciful flights
            And those who dream on beautiful nights
            Dream of beautiful things.

            Beautiful days of for sunshine lazing
            Beautiful skies and shores
            Beautiful days when I can gaze
            In beautiful eyes - like yours.

            Our lives tick by like pendulum swings
            Poor little things, puppets on strings
            Life is full of beautiful things
            Beautiful people too

NEWLEY.   *(Cont)* Beautiful people like you.

The song ends. JOAN takes back the baby.

JOAN.   You see? You weren't stuck for words at all.

NEWLEY.   They were Brickman's.

JOAN.   But you meant them.

NEWLEY.   Oh yes.

JOAN.   I'll make a father of you yet, Newley.

JOAN exits with the baby.

DEVIL.   You never saw it.

NEWLEY.   What's that?

DEVIL.   How beautiful your wife was.

NEWLEY.   I adored her.

DEVIL.   You did?

NEWLEY.   Unfortunately I adored a lot of other women at the same time.

DEVIL.   A restless heart.

NEWLEY.   A restless something. *(Shouts off)* Bromide for Mr. Newley, bromide for Mr. Newley.

DEVIL.   You were always looking for something else.

NEWLEY.   Like Glocca Morra, it was always somewhere just over there.

DEVIL.   You didn't write that one.

NEWLEY.   Which one?

DEVIL.   *How Are Things In Glocca Morra.*

NEWLEY.   I think after my Irish accent in *Doctor Doolittle* I would have been lynched if I had. Brickman wrote the songs for that one.

DEVIL.   You didn't enjoy Doolittle.

NEWLEY.   No, working with Rex Harrison was like wrestling a cobra. Things could get ugly.

DEVIL.   He called you a guttersnipe.

NEWLEY.   Why not, I was.

DEVIL.   And a jumped up Jew-boy.

NEWLEY.   *(Sharp)* Then he won't see heaven.

DEVIL.   He didn't. Mind you, during *My Fair Lady*, he called Julie Andrews the 'c' word.

NEWLEY.   People in glass houses.

REX HARRISON enters, dressed as Doctor Doolittle.

REX.   It wasn't personal.

NEWLEY.   It wasn't?

REX.   I called everyone the 'c' word.

NEWLEY.   Julie Andrews is the nicest person on the planet.

REX.   Yet so common with it.

NEWLEY.   You were such a snob, Rex.

REX.   Undoubtedly.

NEWLEY.   Sneering at all those around you.

REX.   Indubitably.

NEWLEY.   Why?

REX.   Because I could.

NEWLEY.   *Doctor Doolittle* was a famous flop, it bankrupt the studio that made it.

REX.   I blame the animals.

NEWLEY. It was *Doctor Doolittle*.

REX. So?

NEWLEY. It was about a man who talked to bloody animals.

REX. They could have made the film without them, that's all I'm saying. That parrot nearly had my eye out, though its swearing did improve. By the time it went home it knew the 'c' word apparently.

NEWLEY. What about the push-me-pull-you?

REX. A jumped up llama with a second head up its own arse.

NEWLEY. The chimp?

REX. A chronic self-abuser, of the Robert Morley variety.

NEWLEY. The snail?

REX. A mechanical monstrosity.

NEWLEY. You're right, you don't like anything.

REX. Possibly.

DEVIL. You drove your 3rd wife to drink, Rex.

REX. Nonsense, she was a Celt, she was born drunk.

DEVIL. Why did you marry her?

REX. She was a force of nature, even when six sheets to the wind, on all fours and barking like a dog.

NEWLEY. You're a strange man.

REX. I am a genius; we live by no rules but our own. *(Yells)* Lisa, where's my slippers?

REX HARRISON exits.

NEWLEY. He put the 'ego' in egomania.

DEVIL. You weren't far behind.

NEWLEY. I had to love myself. No-one else would.

DEVIL.	Everyone loved you, Newley.
NEWLEY.	But I could never believe it.
DEVIL.	Why's that?
NEWLEY.	You tell me, Doctor Freud.
DEVIL.	I would if I could.
NEWLEY.	I was a paramount egoist, forever watching myself.
DEVIL.	Who isn't?
NEWLEY.	Always aware of myself and the impression I made entering a room. I was searingly aware of being liked and disliked. Why did I find life so ugly at times?
DEVIL.	Life is ugly. Didn't you read the newspapers?
NEWLEY.	Suppose a man grows up with no father and a working class mother.
DEVIL.	A man like you?
NEWLEY.	Precisely; the kid needs all the affection he can get. He works for it. He was born with an engaging little face and nothing more. So he uses his cuteness to get love. It's a device. The process carries through his life into maturity. He sharpens and hones that ability until it is an art. He uses it as the key to something he never had. It is a craving. Acting when you boil it down, is just a plea for approval for love, I acted out Anthony Newley all my life.
DEVIL.	Have you finished?
NEWLEY.	Not yet.

NEWLEY sings: 'Life Is A Woman.'

Life Is A Woman

NEWLEY.	Life, life is a woman An endless surprise Always opening up your heart And closing your eyes Bending your brain Showering you with sunshine

NEWLEY.   *(Cont)* Love and pain
Just like a woman
Life changes each day
Holds you closely to her heart
Then throws you away
What can you say?
Guess its one more game
We have to play
And like a woman
Life can save your soul
With a kiss, one gentle kiss
And all the anger, all the fear
All the pain and sadness disappears
Life being a woman
Will never give in
Takes a special kind of fool
To think he can win
Who wants to win?
Life is a woman
Life is a woman
And if she smiles on you
A woman is your life.

The song ends.

DEVIL.   Where were we?

NEWLEY.   Before we were so rudely interrupted?

DEVIL.   Time to talk about your movie.

NEWLEY.   The one that flopped naturally.

DEVIL.   The one that destroyed your movie career overnight.

NEWLEY.   I wrote, directed and starred in it.

DEVIL.   A fool's folly.

NEWLEY.   It has a cult following. *(Laughs)* I have, after all, been a cult for years.

DEVIL.   It's title?

NEWLEY.   *Can Hieronymus Merkin Ever Forget Mercy Humppe & Find True Happiness. (Beat)* Catchy isn't it?

DEVIL.   Recently voted the worst movie title in film history.

NEWLEY.   It was the 60's, self indulgence was the norm, what can I tell you?

DEVIL.   In it you decided to strip your soul bare -

NEWLEY.   Too bare.

DEVIL.   You discussed your illegitimacy -

NEWLEY.   Well, everyone loves a bastard.

DEVIL.   Your wartime evacuation, your success as a child actor, your shotgun marriage, the torment of losing a child in that marriage -

NEWLEY.   The cows of pathos were well and truly milked.

DEVIL.   And you merry contempt for Hollywood -

NEWLEY.   It's a sugar coated amusement park, an endless round of parties where you park your intellect by the door and dive into a rancid pool of small talk.

DEVIL.   And you wonder why the Hollywood reviewers turned on you?

NEWLEY.   I wanted Brickman to write the songs with me. He refused. He thought the movie was an exercise in megalomania. So did the critics.

DEVIL.   They had a point.

NEWLEY.   In hindsight but hindsight always was a smug berk. I was looking inside myself, trying to find answers.

DEVIL.   To what?

NEWLEY.   Myself. Milton Berle was in it. He was asked -

The Jewish-American comic MILTON BERLE enters, smoking a cigar.

BERLE.   What's the film about? It's about two hours.

BERLE exits.

NEWLEY.   My children played the children in the film -

JOAN enters.

JOAN.   I played a variation of me.

NEWLEY.   'Polyester Poontang.'

JOAN.   The faithful, adoring wife: dragging you down into domestic tedium.

NEWLEY.   I was trying to be honest.

JOAN.   It was a public humiliation.

NEWLEY.   I never thought you'd leave me.

JOAN.   Neither did I.

NEWLEY.   You were never a drudge.

JOAN.   I was way too glamorous for that, darling.

NEWLEY.   I know that.

JOAN.   I put my career on hold for you.

NEWLEY.   I needed to be mothered.

JOAN.   You had your mother to do that.

NEWLEY.   One mother was never enough.

JOAN.   You wonder why I left you?

NEWLEY.   Why did you leave me by the way?

JOAN.   One floozy too many.

NEWLEY.   *(American voice)* I shot a floozy once in my pyjamas.

JOAN.   The jokes wore thin, Tony.

NEWLEY.   And you stopped laughing.

JOAN.   What was there to laugh at?

NEWLEY.   It wasn't you, it was me.

JOAN.   That doesn't help.

NEWLEY.   No.

JOAN.   I stuck it out as long as I could.

NEWLEY.   I'm sorry.

JOAN.   Sorry is easy, Tony; you have to work at love.

JOAN exits.

DEVIL.   You lost the love of your life.

NEWLEY.   Yes.

DEVIL.   But never tried to stop her going.

NEWLEY.   No.

DEVIL.   Why?

NEWLEY.   You expect me to have all the answers.

DEVIL.   If not you, then who?

DEVIL begins to exit.

NEWLEY.   Where you going?

DEVIL.   Time for your soliloquy.

The DEVIL exits.

NEWLEY.   What am I, Hamlet? *(To himself)* More like Yorick.

The lights dim to a spotlight. NEWLEY sings 'Who Can I Turn To?'

Who Can I Turn To?

NEWLEY.   Who can I turn to when nobody needs me?
             My heart wants to know and so I must go where destiny leads me
             With no star to guide me and no one beside me
             I'll go on my way and, after the day, the darkness will hide me

             And maybe tomorrow I'll find what I'm after
             I'll throw off my sorrow, beg, steal, or borrow my share of laughter
             With you I could learn to, with you what a new day
             But who can I turn to if you turn away?

40

NEWLEY. *(Cont)* With you I could learn to, with you what a new day
But who can I turn to if you turn away?
Who can I turn to when nobody needs me?
My heart wants to know and so I must go where destiny leads me
With no star to guide me and no one beside me
I'll go on my way and, after the day, the darkness will hide me.

And maybe tomorrow I'll find what I'm after
I'll throw off my sorrow, beg, steal, or borrow my share of laughter
With you I could learn to, with you what a new day
But who can I turn to if you turn away?

With you I could learn to, with you what a new day
But who can I turn to if you turn away?

The song ends. The lights fade to black.

End of Act One.

Act Two

Lights rise on the same: a circus ring.

A spotlight on: NEWLEY. He sings: 'Once In A Lifetime'

Once In A Lifetime

NEWLEY.   Just once in a lifetime
There's one special moment
One wonderful moment
When fate takes your hand
And this is the moment
My once in a lifetime
When I can explore
A new and exciting land.

For once in my lifetime
I feel like a giant
I soar like an eagle
As though I had wings
For this is my moment
My destiny calls me
And though it may be just once in my lifetime
I'm gonna do great things.

Just once in a lifetime
There's one special moment
One wonderful moment
When fate takes your hand
And this is the moment
My once in a lifetime
When I can explore
A new and exciting land.

Just once in my lifetime
I feel like a giant
I soar like an eagle
As though I had wings
For this is my moment
My destiny calls me
And though it may be just once in my lifetime
I'm gonna do great things.

The song ends. The lights rise and DEVIL enters.

NEWLEY. And where have you been?

DEVIL. Ciggie break.

NEWLEY. So the tobacco companies really are the devil's spawn?

DEVIL. What do you think?

NEWLEY. *(To audience)* Who knew?

DEVIL. Where were we?

NEWLEY. My film with the silly name.

DEVIL. Ah, yes, after *Hieronymus Melkin* flopped the phone stopped ringing.

NEWLEY. Over-night.

DEVIL. Without Joan and the kids you lost your stability.

NEWLEY. Adrift in the psychobabble of La-La Land.

DEVIL. Then Vegas came calling.

NEWLEY. A golden finger, beckoning me with gold.

DEVIL. Newley the crooner was born.

NEWLEY. Mr. Showbiz.

DEVIL. Despite the fact you hated the audience.

NEWLEY. 'The monster with the thousand eyes shouting to be fed.'

DEVIL. Hark at Mr. Bitter.

NEWLEY. I was not a natural Vegas entertainer.

DEVIL. No cod piece stuffed down your trousers?

NEWLEY. Precisely; but I found self-mockery between the songs and total earnestness during them got me a huge following; I out-sold Tom Jones, the highest paid entertainer to play Vegas.

LESLIE BRICUSSE enters.

NEWLEY. Brickman.

BRICUSSE.   In Vegas you stopped writing songs.

NEWLEY.   I was committed to the performances.

BRICUSSE.   And the lavish lifestyle.

NEWLEY.   The limos.

BRICUSSE.   The hotel suites.

NEWLEY.   The minions hired merely to peel me a grape.

BRICUSSE.   You betrayed your talent.

NEWLEY.   So you kept telling me.

BRICUSSE.   I was your friend, someone had too.

NEWLEY.   No-one likes hearing the truth.

BRICUSSE.   Not when you know it's true.

NEWLEY.   We always like to believe we're the hero of our own movie.

BRICUSSE.   Newberg and Brickman had one last film swansong.

NEWLEY.   *Willy Wonka & The Chocolate Factory.*

BRICUSSE.   If only you'd been Wonka.

NEWLEY.   I was always a bit of a Wonka.

BRICUSSE.   With jokes like that who needs Milton Berle? Sing on, McDuff.

BRICUSEE exits. NEWLEY sings 'Pure Imagination.'

Pure Imagination

NEWLEY.   Come with me and you'll be
In a world of pure imagination
Take a look and you'll see
Into your imagination.

NEWLEY.   We'll begin with a spin
            Travelling in the world of my creation
            What we'll see
            Will defy explanation.

            If you want to view paradise
            Simply look around and view it
            Anything you want to, do it
            Want to change the world?
            There's nothing to it.

            There is no life I know
            To compare with pure imagination
            Living there, you'll be free
            If you truly wish to be.

            If you want to view paradise
            Simply look around and view it
            Anything you want to, do it
            Want to change the world?
            There's nothing to it.

            There is no life I know
            To compare with
            Pure imagination
            Living there you'll be free
            If you truly wish to be.

The song ends. The DEVIL applauds ironically.

DEVIL.   You hated the singing in the movie.

NEWLEY.   I offered to sing *Candy Man* for free. It was so badly done.

DEVIL.   But they refused.

NEWLEY.   An opportunity missed.

DEVIL.   Generations adore it.

NEWLEY.   So I'm picky.

DEVIL.   Sammy Davis recorded it.

NEWLEY.   And gave us another hit.

DEVIL.	No wonder that man had hunched shoulders.
NEWLEY.	Why did he have hunched shoulders?
DEVIL.	Carrying your career like that.
NEWLEY.	*(Laughs)* The hunched shoulders were 'cause he was cringing in case Sinatra hit him. Those were the days though, a smashing fellow.
DEVIL.	What's this, nostalgia?
NEWLEY.	Why not? I was king of the world, top of the charts, best friend's with Sammy Davis Junior, on joking terms with The Beatles, surrounded by celebrities and gorgeous women, awash with money and mansions. Those were the days indeed.
DEVIL.	Nostalgia's a bigger drug than heroin and twice as addictive.
NEWLEY.	Didn't you have any good times?
DEVIL.	Well, there was that time I tried to steal God's chair -
NEWLEY.	You see?
DEVIL.	Hello? I'm joking. Good times, bad times, what's the difference? They come they go: we stay the same. Let me tell you -

The DEVIL sings 'The Good Old Bad Old Days.' The CAST enter dressed as devils and join:

The Good Old Bad Old Days

DEVIL &
CAST. Don't you realise we're living today
I'm happy to say in the good old, bad old days
Taking the breaks and making mistakes
In the good old, bad old ways.

Some people say, they long for the old days
To take them way back when
I'd sooner stay here with the gold days
than go through that again
Seems to me, you're out or you're in
You lose or you win
In these sad glad old days.

DEVIL.	(Cont) You're poor or you're rich
	Who knows which is which anyways
	Were living on time we're having to borrow
	Know one knows if we live to see tomorrow
	Never the less, I guess we've gotta confess
	These are good old, bad old days.

Day to day you either up or you're down
A king or a clown
In the good old, bad old days
It's heaven or hell, hello or farewell
In the good old, bad old days
Looking around the world that surrounds me I think good god forgot about
But I have found one thing that astounds me the worlds still full of love
and I realise that come rain or come shine
That you'll survive all these crazy, mad old days
In war or in peace they do never cease to amaze.

Were living on time we're having to borrow
Know one knows if we live to see tomorrow
People will say when they look back at today
Those were the good old, the good old bad old days.

The song ends. The CAST exit. The DEVIL fights to get his breathe back after an exuberant dance routine.

NEWLEY.	Have you finished?
DEVIL.	I've come over all weary.
NEWLEY.	Showbiz is harder than it looks.
DEVIL.	I'm getting old.
NEWLEY.	How old are you?
DEVIL.	Counting today?
NEWLEY.	Yes.
DEVIL.	Four million, eight hundred and forty seven.
NEWLEY.	Ask a stupid question.
DEVIL.	Where were we?

NEWLEY.	I returned to England, in the early 70's, to appear in the West End.
DEVIL.	The old stamping ground.
NEWLEY.	Doing a show Brickman and I had written called 'The Good Old Bad Old Days.' *(Beat)* There was a devil in it.
DEVIL.	*(Mock guilty)* Never heard of it.
NEWLEY.	You surprise me.

BRICUSSE enters.

BRICUSSE.	We originally called the show: 'It's A Funny Old World We Live In - But The World's Not Entirely To Blame.'
DEVIL.	Catchy.
BRICUSSE.	A modest little saga about Man -
NEWLEY.	Life -
BRICUSSE.	Death -
NEWLEY.	God -
BRICUSSE.	And the Devil -
DEVIL.	I always got the best tunes.
BRICUSSE.	We'd both changed since last we'd worked together.
NEWLEY.	You were always out socially.
BRICUSSE.	You never left your den unless you had too.
NEWLEY.	You loved the public.
BRICUSEE.	*(Laughs)* You wanted to attack them with a flame thrower.
NEWLEY.	I'd come to resent them.
BRICUSSE.	I loved sunny days and sunny people.
NEWLEY.	I lived for the night, a vampire of the cabaret circuit.

BRICUSSE.   Touring with Buddy Hackett -

NEWLEY.   Victor Borge -

BRICUSSE.   Dionne Warwick -

NEWLEY.   Joan Rivers -

BRICUSSE.   Bob Newhart -

NEWLEY.   They were legion. There were days I forgot who I was touring with or even where I was.

BRICUSSE.   Another hotel room -

NEWLEY.   Another stolen towel.

BRICUSSE.   You'd met Dareth.

NEWLEY.   My air hostess.

BRICUSSE.   I thought she'd bring you some peace.

NEWLEY.   She did, for a while; she gave me children, more precious children. I was always at ease with my children. Sometimes it was the only peace I ever knew.

BRICUSSE.   The show lasted nine months in the West End.

NEWLEY.   It seemed like years.

BRICUSSE.   Only to you.

NEWLEY.   I'd lost the ability to do the same thing night after night.

BRICUSSE.   You wouldn't take it to Broadway.

NEWLEY.   I couldn't do it anymore.

BRICUSSE.   I know.

NEWLEY.   I went back to Vegas and took the devil's shilling.

DEVIL.   Don't blame me for Vegas. That hell is man-made.

BRICUSSE.   You let Vegas eat you up.

NEWLEY. And I didn't even scream.

BRICUSSE. Newberg, Newberg, what might have been, what might have been.

BRICUSSE exits.

DEVIL. He does nag so, doesn't he?

NEWLEY. Only because he cared, only because he cared.

DEVIL. You should be like Sinatra and have no regrets.

NEWLEY. Only a man with a skin as thick as a rhino has no regrets.

DEVIL. Ah, you've met Sinatra then?

NEWLEY. My regrets are legion.

NEWLEY sings: 'The Good Things In Life.'

The Good Things In Life

NEWLEY. I have lived, I have loved, I have laughed, I have cried
I have tried to give my life some meaning
I have tried to make it all make sense.

I have made the journey up the mountain and the descents
I have known the bitter taste of sadness
I have fought some pretty hopeless fights
I have lived the loveliest of days and loneliest nights.

I have won, I have lost, I have learned to my cost
That I've crossed and burned too many bridges
If I could go back perhaps I would
Then again I don't take good advice when maybe I should.

But I raise my glass to the good things in life
To a place in the sun where our children can run
To the green of the grass and the love of a wife.

I've been right, I've been wrong, I've been weak; I've been strong
And I long to live in someone's memory and I long to live upon a hill
And it doesn't matter that I ever will.

NEWLEY.   *(Cont)* But I raise my glass to the good things in life
            I am not here for long, but there's time for a song and some wine
            And when time runs away I will look back and say:
            That the good things in life were all mine.

The song ends.

DEVIL.   And then Quilp?

NEWLEY.   For the movies, another Dickens grotesque, I played them so well.

DEVIL.   Then back to the cabaret circuit.

NEWLEY.   Going round and round and round, 'til I was sick.

An enthusiastic AMERICAN AGENT enters.

AGENT.   *(American & fast)* Tony baby, have I got a tour for you: Biloxi on the
            14th, Little Rock on the 15th, Toronto on the 16th, Tel Aviv for Yon
            Kippur, Detroit on the 19th, Belgium on the 23rd, Alcatraz on the 25th,
            Atlantis on the 26th, Brigadoon on the 29th, Babylon on the 30th
            Mordor on the 2nd, Tracey Island on the 5th, Singapore on the 6th,
            Gateshead on the 8th, Saigon on the 9th, back to Vegas to play a Mafia
            Convention on the 11th, Burnley on the 12th, Alaska on the 13th, Little
            Big Horn on the 16th, Valley Forge on the 18th, a Klan rally on the 20th,
            Shangri-La on the 22nd, Stonehenge on the 23rd, Hugh Heffner's
            Jacuzzi on the 24th then back to Nevada for a P.L.O benefit on the
            26th. You'll knock 'em dead, sweetie. Remember to dry clean the tux.
            See you in the V.I.P lounge at Kennedy. Don't ever change. There's a
            lot of love in this room and it's all pointing your way. Got to fly, Wayne
            Newton needs me to iron-press his buttocks before he opens at
            Caesar's Palace.

The AMERICAN AGENT exits.

NEWLEY.   The venues, like the fees, started to get smaller. But I had one creative
            dream left.

CHARLIE CHAPLIN enters, in his familiar tramp guise. He doffs his cap to Newley.

DEVIL.   *(Laughs)* My God, Hitler's escaped, and he's wearing a disguise.

NEWLEY.   Chaplin, I wanted to write a musical about Chaplin.

NEWLEY starts to slow waltz with the actor dressed as CHAPLIN.

DEVIL.   Why Chaplin?

NEWLEY.   He was born dirt poor like me, on the Kennington Road.

DEVIL.   Ah, working class whining, one more time.

NEWLEY.   Why not? We've got a lot to whine about. Charlie's old man had died and left him. His mother was put in a lunatic asylum, almost an orphan. He was put into a workhouse.

DEVIL.   You never saw the inside of a workhouse.

NEWLEY.   What was Rank? He was a child performer, singing for his supper, like me. He made his name and fortune in America, like me.

DEVIL.   And was an infamous womaniser?

NEWLEY.   That too.

DEVIL.   Attacked by the critics in later life like you?

NEWLEY.   Naturally; neither of us had been educated, he wrote songs like me. He was a perfectionist just like me. Littlechap and the Tramp, we were cut from the same cloth.

DEVIL.   Wasn't *Chaplin* the musical where the critics said you drown in your own sentimentality?

NEWLEY.   The very same.

DEVIL.   They said you didn't play Chaplin, you just played Newley.

NEWLEY.   Me and John Wayne both.

DEVIL.   *(Mock surprise)* John Wayne played Anthony Newley?

NEWLEY.   He always played himself, arse. *(Shouts off)* Cab for Satan, cab for Satan.

DEVIL.   They said you were too close to the subject.

NEWLEY.   Maybe, but it wasn't just that. I didn't have the energy any more.

DEVIL.   Energy?

NEWLEY.   Musical theatre, like water polo and war, is a young man's game. But I put my heart and soul into it. It was my lifetime's dream after all. It was supposed to go to Broadway. But it never did.

CHAPLIN and NEWLEY break off dancing. NEWLEY bows, CHAPLIN doffs his cap and exits.

DEVIL.   How did you take it?

NEWLEY.   With great maturity: I locked myself in my bedroom and refused to come out, not even for my Mum.

DEVIL.   Blaming the critics.

NEWLEY.   *(Snaps)* What's a critic but a eunuch at an orgy?

DEVIL.   What did you do after that?

NEWLEY.   I fell back on the success of my youth.

DEVIL.   Weren't you a little old for the Dodger?

NEWLEY.   I toured *Stop The World - I Want To Get Off.*

DEVIL.   An act of desperation?

NEWLEY.   As I found out, I was increasingly unhappy; I didn't want to be married anymore, I felt like I was dying.

DEVIL.   All mortals die, old son.

NEWLEY.   Faster than I should.

DEVIL.   So you threw all dignity to the wind and took up with a nineteen year old?

NEWLEY.   I was fifty-seven and living with my Mum. Allow a man some perks.

DEVIL.   And ran back to England when that ended?

NEWLEY.   It seemed the natural conclusion: the circle of life and all that.

DEVIL.   Back to *Stop The World* one more time?

NEWLEY.   It was my cash cow. It had to be milked.

DEVIL.   The London critics were waiting.

NEWLEY.   Like Comanche waiting to ambush a wagon train, there was blood all over the floor. They'd never forgiven my success in America. It got worse.

Enter GRACIE.

GRACIE.   You were broke.

NEWLEY.   Fashions had changed, Vegas had changed, Newley did not disco.

GRACIE.   Nobody wanted to hear you sing anymore.

NEWLEY.   The millions had gone.

GRACIE.   With the wind, we had to sell everything.

NEWLEY.   All the treasures.

GRACIE.   We ended up living in Esher.

NEWLEY.   *(To the Devil)* Mum and me.

GRACIE.   All the tuxes went.

NEWLEY.   All the cigarette cases, all the trinkets.

GRACIE.   All the trappings of fame.

NEWLEY.   I found myself performing a show in a back room in Islington.

GRACIE.   Doing *Once Upon A Song*.

NEWLEY.   'Guerrilla Theatre' I called it.

GRACIE.   Slumming it I called it.

NEWLEY.   The mighty had fallen.

GRACIE.   The ego had landed.

NEWLEY.   My nadir.

GRACIE.   Rock bottom.

NEWLEY.   Sixteen reviews.

GRACIE.   Fifteen of them bad.

NEWLEY.   I looked like Mr. Toad, they said.

GRACIE.   How could he sink so far? They said.

NEWLEY.   His voice a tedious warble, they said.

GRACIE.   His famous smile an obscene leer, they said.

NEWLEY.   A hunched grotesque, they said.

GRACIE.   A cavorting gnome, they said, the anti-Semitic bastards.

NEWLEY.   *(Laughs)* Mum, just because they didn't like me doesn't mean they were anti-Semitic.

GRACIE.   It's my theory and I'm sticking to it.

GRACIE exits.

DEVIL.   So you were down and out?

NEWLEY.   In Esher and London.

DEVIL.   Didn't George Orwell turn it into a book?

NEWLEY.   If he'd been alive he would.

DEVIL.   What saved you?

NEWLEY.   The usual suspects: Dickens via Brickman.

DEVIL.   Fagin?

NEWLEY.   Scrooge, love, Scrooge. Face it, I had the deep pockets.

BRICUSSE enters.

BRICUSSE.   You were just a stage actor this time.

NEWLEY.   For the first time in thirty-five years.

BRICUSSE.   It was made for you.

NEWLEY.   I'd been preparing for that role all my life.

BRICUSSE.   You were ready, one last time you pulled out all the stops.

NEWLEY.   You always came along at the right time.

BRICUSSE.   What are friends for? Sing Lofty, sing.

I'll Begin Again

NEWLEY.   I'll begin again
I will build my life
I will live to know
I fulfilled my life
I'll begin today, throw away the past
And the future I build
Will be something that will last
I will take the time
That I have left to live
And I'll give it all
That I have left to give
I will live my days
For my fellow men
And I'll live in praise
Of that moment when
I was able to begin again.
I'll begin again
I will change my fate
I will show the world
That it is not too late
I will never stop
While I still have time
'Till I stand at the top
Of the mountain I must climb
I will start anew
I will make amends
And I will make quite certain
That the story ends
On a note of hope
On a strong amen
And I'll thank the world
And remember when
I was able to begin again
I'll begin again.

The song ends.

DEVIL.   Success plucked from the jaws of defeat?

NEWLEY.   One last triumph.

DEVIL.   And then the cancer.

NEWLEY.   I went down fighting.

DEVIL.   Trying to write a musical on Richard III.

NEWLEY.   Indeed. *(Laughs)* I was going to call it *Who's Got The Hump?*

DEVIL.   You never finished it.

NEWLEY.   I never got the time, there were so many dreams, projects to finish, there just wasn't enough time.

DEVIL.   You faded away.

NEWLEY.   My new career as a 'soap' actor curtailed.

DEVIL.   A mass audience waiting.

NEWLEY.   What might have been.

DEVIL.   What might have been.

NEWLEY.   Death's what happens to you in between making plans.

DEVIL.   And your last words?

NEWLEY.   'It's all a book isn't it?'

DEVIL.   What was the title of the book?

NEWLEY.   'Anthony Newley & How To Achieve It.'

DEVIL.   *(Laughs)* Ah, you always were the joker in the pack.

NEWLEY.   You're telling me.

The CAST enter and sing a reprise of 'The Joker' with the DEVIL.

The Joker (Reprise)

DEVIL &
CAST.   There's always a Joker in the pack
There's always a cardboard clown
The poor painted fool falls on his back
And everyone laughs when he's down.

DEVIL & CAST.	There's always a funny man in the game But he's only funny by mistake But everyone laughs at him, just the same They don't see his painted heart break. They don't care as long as there is a jester, just a fool As foolish as he can be There's always a Joker, that's a rule But fate deals the hand and you see The Joker is you. There's always a funny man in the game But he's only funny by mistake But everyone laughs at him, just the same They don't see his painted heart break. They don't care as long as there is a jester, just a fool As foolish as he can be There's always a Joker, that's a rule But fate deals the hand and you can see The Joker is you The Joker is you The Joker is you.

The CAST exit.

NEWLEY.	Well, there's no need to rub it in.
DEVIL.	I'm the Devil: it's my job to rub it in.
NEWLEY.	I hadn't thought of that.
DEVIL.	Why did you ask me here?
NEWLEY.	You know full well.
DEVIL.	Oh, I don't you think there's a place for you down below.
NEWLEY.	Why not?
DEVIL.	I'm not taking someone just because he doesn't think he's worthy of heaven, that's not how it works.
NEWLEY.	It doesn't?

DEVIL.   There's millions of you. If I took you all I wouldn't be able to move down below for the massed ranks of the self-loathing. It'd be standing room only.

NEWLEY.   Does it matter?

DEVIL.   Of course it matters. I only take the wicked of heart.

NEWLEY.   Wasn't I that?

DEVIL.   Not you. You were a better man than you ever let on.

NEWLEY.   I was a basket case.

DEVIL.   Hey, nobody's perfect.

JOAN enters with BRICUSSE.

NEWLEY.   They're ganging up on me now.

JOAN.   It's time, Newley.

NEWLEY.   For what?

BRICUSSE. You know what, Newberg.

JOAN.   You were a joy to know, Newley.

BRICUSSE. *(Laughs)* And a royal pain in the arse.

JOAN.   A loving father but a lousy husband.

BRICUSSE. The best friend a man could have and sometimes the worst.

JOAN.   A mass of contradictions.

BRICUSSE. The brother I never had.

JOAN.   The soul-mate I always missed.

BRICUSSE. You threw away your career.

JOAN.   You threw away your love.

BRICUSSE. But you were Newberg.

JOAN.   You were Tony.

BRICUSSE.   Littlechap and Cocky -

JOAN.   And Dodger, the greatest Dodger of them all.

BRICUSSE.   They'll only ever be one Newley.

JOAN.   *(Laughs)* Thank God.

DEVIL.   I'll be crying in a minute. Can we reach a conclusion here?

JOAN.   Yes, quit stalling, Newley, you know it's time.

NEWLEY.   For what?

JOAN.   Your Sermon on the Mount.

NEWLEY.   Not that song.

BRICUSSE.   You never sang it the same way twice.

JOAN.   It was your statement to the world.

BRICUSSE.   Close the show, Newberg.

JOAN.   Stop the world, one more time.

NEWLEY.   Must I?

BRICUSSE.   Every fool must have his moment.

JOAN.   And no fool ever sang it better.

He looks from BRICUSSE to JOAN and back. He smiles and finally nods in surrender.

They watch as NEWLEY sings: 'What Kind Of Fool Am I?'

The lights gradually dim until there is only a spotlight on Newley's face.

What Kind Of Fool Am I?

NEWLEY.   What kind of fool I am, who never fell in love?
              It seems that I'm the only one I have been thinking of
              What kind of man is this? An empty shell, a lonely cell
              In which an empty heart must dwell?

60

NEWLEY.   *(Cont)* What kind of lips are these?
               that lied with every kiss?
               That whispered empty words of love that left me alone like this?
               Why can't I fall in love like any other man?
               And maybe then I'll know what kind of fool I am.

               What kind of clown am I? What do I know of life?
               Why can't I cast away the mask of play and live my life?
               Why can't I fall in love, till I don't give a damn?
               And maybe then I'll know what kind of fool I am.

               What kind of fool I am, who never fell in love?
               It seems that I'm the only one I have been thinking of
               What kind of man is this? An empty shell, a lonely cell
               In which an empty heart must dwell?

               What kind of lips are these?
               that lied with every kiss?
               That whispered empty words of love that left me alone like this?
               Why can't I fall in love like any other man?
               And maybe then I'll know what kind of fool I am.

               What kind of clown am I? What do I know of life?
               Why can't I cast away the mask of play and live my life?
               Why can't I fall in love, till I don't give a damn?
               And maybe then I'll know what kind of fool I am.

*JOAN, BRICUSSE, the DEVIL and CAST melt into the shadows as the lights dim
to a spotlight on Newley's face as he sings.*

At the final dramatic note of the song the spotlight - snaps off.

The lights rise, the CAST enter, bow and exit once more.

The End

© Roy Smiles 2021.

Printed in Great Britain
by Amazon

62044475R20037